LEVI
STRAUSS

Blue Jean Tycoon

Meish Goldish

44044

ROURKE ENTERPRISES,INC.
VERO BEACH, FLORIDA 32964

A Blackbirch Graphics book.

Library of Congress Cataloging-in-Publication Data

Goldish, Meish.
    Levi Strauss / by Meish Goldish.
      p.   cm. — (Made in America)
    Includes index.
    Summary: Traces the life of the immigrant Jewish peddler who went on to found Levi Strauss & Co., the world's first and largest manufacturer of denim jeans.
    ISBN 0-86592-070-2
    1. Strauss, Levi, 1829–1902—Juvenile literature. 2. Business-men—United States—Juvenile literature. 3. Levi Strauss and Company—History—Juvenile literature. [1. Strauss, Levi, 1829–1902. 2. Businessmen. 3. Levi Strauss and Company—History.] I. Title. II. Series.
HD9940.U4S793 1993
338.7'689'092—dc20
[B]   93-11997
                                           CIP
                                           AC

Contents

The Early Years

Hard work could make you rich.

Levi's jeans. No doubt you've heard of them. Their ads can be seen on television, in magazines, and on billboards. Perhaps you're even wearing a pair right now. One thing is certain: Levi's are the most famous jeans in the world. They're sold in 70 countries. In countries where the jeans are not available, people are often willing to pay high prices to anyone who can supply them.

How did Levi's become so popular? Whose idea were they? When were they first made? The answers to these questions lie in the fascinating story of their creator, Levi Strauss.

Opposite: With creativity, kindness, and determination, Levi Strauss altered the course of American business forever.

Taking Over Father's Business

Levi Strauss was born in 1829 in the small
village of Buttenheim, at the base of the
Bavarian Alps, in what is now Germany.
His parents, Hirsch and Rebecca Strauss,
named their son Loeb—a name that comes
from the Hebrew word Lev, meaning
"heart." Loeb was the youngest child of six.
From his first marriage, Hirsch Strauss
had four children—Jacob, Jonas, Louis,
and Mathilde. After his wife died, Hirsch
married again and had two more children,
Fanny and Loeb.

Loeb's father sold dry goods, such as
cloth, lace, buttons, needles, pins, scissors,
and thread, for a living. In Central and
Eastern Europe, many Jewish merchants
like Hirsch Strauss were peddlers. They
carried their goods from town to town in
large, heavy sacks. They stopped at each
house along the way, hoping to sell a few
items before moving on.

Hirsch Strauss died of lung disease in
1845. His youngest child, Loeb, was only
16 years old. What would the Strausses do
now without their father? How would they
survive? Young Loeb had few choices. He
took his father's large sacks and began
to peddle dry goods in Buttenheim. After

During the early 1800s, many Jewish merchants of Central and Eastern Europe were street peddlers. Levi started peddling when he was only 16 years old.

all, the family still had to eat. But two of Loeb's half brothers, Jonas and Louis, had other ideas. They packed their belongings and headed out for America, where they believed hard work could make you rich. They also thought that Jews would be treated better there than in Germany.

A New Life

In 1847, just two years after Jonas and Louis's departure, Rebecca Strauss decided to go to America, as well. She got passports for herself, Mathilde, Fanny, and Loeb. (Records do not indicate what became of the oldest brother, Jacob.) The Strausses now faced a brighter future. But getting to America would not be easy. The family first had to travel by carriage to Hamburg, one of Germany's port cities. From there they would begin a long voyage across the North Sea and the Atlantic Ocean.

Mrs. Strauss knew she could not take much with her to America. She packed only a few of the family's belongings, plus some kosher food that might not be available on the ship.

At the port of Hamburg, long lines of travelers carried their bundles onto the ship. Rooms on the ship were generally dirty and crowded. There was little fresh water or food. The Strausses traveled in steerage, the cheapest fare, which meant riding in the lowest part of the vessel. In the damp, windowless quarters below, there was hardly room to stand up. Space had to be shared with dozens of other passengers. People slept on hard bunk beds.

Europeans who hoped to make the journey to America during the mid-1800s had to first brave the crowded seaports at home. Here, passengers gather at the port of Hamburg on the Elbe River in Germany.

During the uncomfortable voyage, many passengers became seasick. Some grew seriously ill and died. Doctors on board were rare. Despite these rough conditions, the travelers never lost hope. America, they believed, held far more promise for them than life in their homeland.

After 42 days at sea, the ship finally reached New York. Loeb and his family rushed on deck to look for Jonas and Louis, who were to meet them. They did not see the two young men. But what they did see was a wondrous sight to behold.

Hundreds of people scurried along the docking area. Workers moved quickly to unload cargo from the ships from Japan, France, and England. They carried sacks of coffee, bolts of silk, and other merchandise.

Loeb and his family could only look on in amazement. They hardly believed they were about to set foot in America, their busy new home. But passengers on board were not allowed to just walk off the boat and into the streets of New York. First they had to be "processed," or officially entered into the formal record book kept by the U.S. government.

Long lines of passengers stood patiently at Ward's Island in the East River of New York City. Government officials questioned each person and wrote down information. "Do you have relatives in America?" "Do you have any diseases?" "Do you have work lined up?" Most passengers, like Loeb, had trouble understanding the questions. They spoke only Yiddish—a combination of German and Hebrew—while the officials spoke mainly in English.

"What is your name?" an official asked Loeb. The frightened young man barely understood. "Loeb Strauss," he mumbled. The official may have misunderstood the reply. He jotted a note in the record book and said to Loeb, "Your name is Levi

The U.S. government used Ward's Island, located in the
East River of New York City, to process many new
immigrants like Levi during the mid-nineteenth century.

Strauss." Now Loeb had not only a new home in America but a new name as well.

Finally, Levi, his mother, and sisters were able to leave the dock. Just then they heard Jonas and Louis calling to them. In the vast crowd, they managed to spot one another. Soon Mathilde, Fanny, and Levi were hugging the brothers they hadn't seen in two years. At last the Strauss family was together again.

Rebecca couldn't get over how different the older boys looked. Their clothes were not the clothes of their Bavarian village, but of America. Jonas and Louis explained the living arrangements they had made for the family. Their mother and sisters would stay with relatives on New York's Lower East Side, where many Jews from Europe had settled. Levi would stay with his brothers in a rooming house—a building with furnished rooms for rent. Levi would also help his brothers with their work. Like their late father, Jonas and Louis had gone into the dry-goods business.

Everything was new and exciting for Levi and his family. America was "the golden land." It held the promise of honest work, a good living, and a rewarding life.

2

Getting Started in America

Levi Strauss knew he could succeed as a peddler in New York.

In the 1840s, New York's Lower East Side was bustling with people who had come from Europe. Many of them were Jewish. New York offered a variety of business opportunities, but there were still problems to deal with. For one thing, few of these foreigners were able to speak or understand English. They could not just walk into a company and apply for a job. As a result, many went into business for themselves, as peddlers.

The Lower East Side was filled with peddlers' pushcarts. From the streets came the merchants' cries: "Fresh fruit!" "Hats!"

"Pots and pans!" Customers browsed, passing from one cart to the next. Peddlers might charge a penny or a nickel for items such as shoelaces, pencils, or pickles.

Peddling on New York's Streets

Levi Strauss knew he could succeed as a peddler in New York. After all, he had done the same kind of work in Buttenheim. But Levi lacked money to begin his business.

Fortunately, Levi's older brothers Jonas and Louis were eager to help out. They guided Levi to the large supply house where peddlers bought their goods. They helped him pick out the items he needed.

Levi did not have enough money to buy a cart to hold all his goods. Instead, he wore a heavy pack on his back. Loaded, it weighed as much as 100 pounds. On the street, Levi began to make a living. He also began to learn English and to understand American ways of doing business.

Business was slow but steady. Levi saw that the streets of New York City were filled with peddlers. He thought he might do better where there was less competition, so he started selling his wares as far away as Pelham, New York, about 15 miles north of the city. On Monday morning he would

New York City's Lower East Side was a bustling place in the 1840s. Most of the Jewish immigrants that arrived from Europe made their first homes there.

pack up a week's worth of goods. All week he'd go from house to house, offering his dry goods. At night he usually slept in barns or stables. By Friday evening, Levi would return home to observe the Jewish Sabbath with his family.

As the months passed, Levi managed to save more and more money. At the same time, his brothers were also becoming more successful. By 1848, Jonas had his own dry-goods store on Division Street. Three years later, Jonas and Louis became partners in an even larger store on Houston Street.

Meanwhile, changes were happening for the rest of the Strauss family as well. Levi's sister Fanny married David Stern, another new American from Europe. She and David decided to move to St. Louis, Missouri. Levi's other sister, Mathilde, also married. Together, she and her husband, William Sahlein, left New York and headed west.

A Welcome in Kentucky

Levi wished to see more of America. In 1848, he decided to move to Kentucky and live with a relative there. For someone in Levi's situation, this was a brave decision to make. Kentucky was largely an unexplored frontier at the time. Pioneers often had conflicts with Native-American tribes living in the area. There were stories of peddlers who had been murdered along the roads or attacked by wild animals. But Levi was willing to take the risk.

The trip to Louisville was not a very easy one. After getting settled, he took on the challenge of peddling dry goods in the Kentucky hills. Levi set a goal for himself.

Every day he would try to cover 10 miles
and sell three dollars worth of wares. Some
days he succeeded. Other days he did not.
Nevertheless, Levi continued to work hard.

Happily, Levi discovered that southern
families treated peddlers from the East with
a special respect. Peddlers brought news of
neighbors and of doings in nearby towns.
Religious southerners were particularly
interested in peddlers because they knew
that many peddlers were Hebrews who
clung to traditional ways. They were eager
to know more about the peddlers' heritage
and customs. When Levi visited families,
he would describe to them his religious
upbringing in Europe and the traditions
that Jews followed.

Levi soon discovered that peddlers were
also welcomed by the Native Americans.
Many tribes did not trust pioneers who
came to the area. But peddlers were known
as nonviolent people. They came only with
their wares, not with weapons for battle.
Besides, peddlers were merely passing
through. They did not plan to settle on the
Indians' land.

Day after day, Levi carried his heavy
sacks through the hills, prairies, and villages
of Kentucky. After selling some of his

As a peddler in Kentucky from 1848 to 1853, Levi polished his business skills and gained a reputation as an honest businessperson.

wares, Levi found his load not lighter, but heavier. That was because some customers paid Levi with goods instead of money.

Levi Strauss stayed in Kentucky from 1848 to 1853. During that time, he built up a small business and a reputation for honesty. By this time, Levi could speak and understand English fairly well. But Levi had even bigger plans and dreams.

Another Move

While Levi was in the South, word began to quickly spread across the country about the

18

discovery of gold in California. Swarms of adventurous and hopeful Californians headed for the hills and streams where the gold lay. Thousands more traveled from other states and territories to seek their fortunes in the rush.

Levi decided that he, too, would find prosperity in the West. But Levi wasn't dreaming of becoming a gold miner. He had another idea. He reasoned that where there were miners, there was a need for tents, pots and pans, blankets, and other items.

Levi wasn't the only family member who was thinking of California. By now, his sister Fanny and her husband were already living in San Francisco. They had started a business there in 1850. They wanted Levi to come out and join them.

In 1853, Levi packed his belongings and returned to New York from Kentucky. There he announced to his family his plans of moving to California. Jonas and Louis asked him to stay to help them run their business, but Levi knew he had to take the risk of going out West. He wished his mother and brothers a fond farewell and prepared for what would probably be the most difficult journey of his life.

3

California Boom

Levi had discovered his own special gold mine.

     In 1853, traveling from New York to California was difficult. Levi had a choice of three routes. First, he could ride a train to the Mississippi River, then cross the remaining thousands of miles by wagon. If the wagon could not make it over the rocky terrain, he would have to walk.

     Levi's second choice was to take a steamer ship to Panama. There he could cross the land by foot until he reached the Pacific Ocean. He would have to board a second steamer in order to eventually reach California. But this choice, too, required both long and uncomfortable hiking.

A Difficult Journey

Levi took his third choice. He rode a clipper ship all the way down the eastern coasts of North America and South America. The ship went around Cape Horn and then headed up the western coast to California. Although this was the longest route in terms of mileage and time, it was the safest.

Levi's journey, like the one he had taken to America six years earlier, was very hard. Violent storms threatened to tear apart the ship during the voyage. On board were many kinds of people—farmers, doctors, peddlers, and laborers—all sharing dreams of prosperity. They had heard stories of gold miners who became millionaires overnight. In fact, almost none of these stories were true. Most people were lucky to find even a few hundred dollars' worth of gold.

After four hard months, Levi's ship reached San Francisco's Long Wharf. There, hundreds of ships had been abandoned by crews who had headed out in search of gold. Almost everyone had "gold fever."

Seizing an Opportunity

Because of the gold rush, San Francisco was growing at an astounding rate. In 1850, the year California became a state,

San Francisco had about 25,000 people in it. Three years later, its population reached almost 70,000. New hotels, stores, and shops sprang up week after week. Unfortunately, the rapid increase in population also brought a rapid rise in crime. Criminals did not hesitate to rob and kill miners who had found gold in the hills.

Outside the city, fortune seekers worked and lived in "diggings." Finding gold was difficult, and it took its toll on both the miners and their clothing.

Before Levi Strauss even stepped off his ship, he discovered how well a peddler in California might do. Nearly his entire stock of goods was bought right on board! All he had left were a few bolts (large pieces) of canvas. Levi had brought the tough cloth to sell to miners for tents and wagon covers.

At the wharf, Levi was met by his sister Fanny and his brother-in-law David. The couple was delighted to have Levi move in with them. They offered him work at David's dry-goods store in San Francisco.

In the store, David and Levi sold cloth, canvas, blankets, cups, dishes, and other items. They also sold shirts and pants. Most of the merchandise arrived by ship from New York. Levi's brothers, Jonas and

When Levi arrived at San Francisco's port area in the mid-1850s, he found hundreds of ships abandoned by their crews. Most had gone off in search of gold.

Louis, supplied large bolts of canvas and other fabric to the California store.

Levi and David developed an efficient system for running their operation. In the days before a ship was due, the two would sleep in the store so they could prepare the shelves for the new merchandise. They paid a young boy to stand on the roof of one of San Francisco's tallest buildings to watch for incoming ships. Once the ship arrived, Levi would rush to the wharf. There an auction was held. Merchants would bid for many of the goods on board.

Levi knew exactly what he wanted to buy at each auction. Then he and David would sell the wares at their store. Little by little, their business grew. In 1856, the two men moved into an even larger store. They sold both retail and wholesale. (Retail means selling small amounts of goods to individual customers. Wholesale means selling large amounts of goods to owners of other stores.)

Levi Strauss & Co.

Soon Levi and David were equal partners in the business, along with Jonas and Louis in New York. However, they could not call their company "Strauss Brothers." That name had already been taken by another firm in San Francisco. The family agreed that Levi had the best mind for business, so they called themselves "Levi Strauss & Co."

Sales were brisk in the new San Francisco store, but Levi wanted to grow even bigger. Living up to his reputation, he soon found another way to increase business. He knew that many miners outside the city could not easily get back to San Francisco for fresh supplies, so Levi himself went out to the diggings. Using a horse and wagon, he peddled his wares from camp to camp, just as he had done in Buttenheim, New York, and Kentucky.

Jeans: An Accidental Discovery

No one knows for sure exactly when Levi got the idea for his now-famous "Levi's jeans," but a popular legend goes like this: One day in the diggings, Levi met a miner and offered to sell him canvas for a tent. The miner didn't need a tent, but he asked if Levi had any rugged overalls to sell him. He explained that his clothing didn't last very long, since he spent many hours on his knees panning near streams.

Suddenly, Levi had a brainstorm! He told the miner he would deliver his overalls in a few days. Then he went off to find a tailor to cut his canvas fabric into a pair of work pants. The miner was very pleased with this rugged new clothing. Soon other miners were asking for the same canvas pants. Levi had accidentally discovered his own special gold mine.

Levi rushed off a letter to Jonas and Louis, asking them to ship more canvas. Since they were out of canvas at the time, denim was sent instead. Denim, a heavy cotton material, came from the French town of Nimes. For years, sailors in Genoa, Italy, had used blue denim for pants. Because people from Genoa are known as Genoese, the pants were called "jeans."

Word about Levi's new denim pants spread rapidly throughout California. Travelers soon brought news of the pants to other parts of the West and Southwest. Cowboys were interested in the denim pants because they were tough enough to last during long rides in the saddle. Railroad workers and farmers who lived west of the Mississippi were also among the first to ask for a pair of "Levi's."

Farmers, railroad workers, and miners were some of the first people to appreciate Levi's jeans. Here, the accidental inventor himself—Levi Strauss—distributes his new product to some California miners.

Levi and David could hardly keep up with the demand for their new creation. Their business was growing by leaps and bounds, but it wasn't from jeans alone. Miners began bringing their families to San Francisco to settle, so Levi Strauss & Co. was soon selling dresses and children's clothing. Levi himself gained a reputation in and around California as a dependable and honest businessperson.

Business in a Changing America

Whenever Levi saw a chance for growth, he grabbed it.

As the 1850s drew to a close, Levi Strauss & Co. continued to thrive. The store was open daily—6 A.M. until 6 P.M.—except Sunday. Aside from selling their American-made products, the company began to import fine linens and lace from countries such as Ireland, Italy, and Belgium.

Many changes took place in the United States during this time. These changes affected American business in several ways, some good and some bad.

Opposite: By the late 1850s, Levi's rugged "jeans" were a common sight on California's miners. As more and more workers used these pants, they gained a national reputation for long-lasting toughness and value.

Improved Communications Help Levi's Company

In 1860, a new type of mail service called the Pony Express began. A relay team of horses could rush letters from California to St. Joseph, Missouri, in only nine days. There, the mail was put on a train for New York, where it arrived five days later. Levi Strauss could send letters to his brothers' store in the East in record time.

Then, in 1861, the Pacific Telegraph made it possible to wire messages from coast to coast in an instant. Levi could

The growth of the railroad industry in the 1860s was a great development for Levi Strauss. With fast, direct transportation, Levi's merchandise was distributed much faster and to a wider market.

place orders with his New York suppliers immediately.

Just as the telegraph had helped Levi's business along, so, too, did the railroad system. On May 10, 1869, the Union Pacific railroad tracks and the Central Pacific tracks were joined at Promontory Summit, Utah. Trains could now roll from coast to coast, enabling shipments to go from New York to California without going around South America. Because of this rail link, Levi's merchandise could travel a lot faster.

Surviving a War and an Earthquake

While the 1860s brought changes that gave Levi's business a boost, there were also serious problems in America.

In 1861, the Civil War, in which the North fought the South over the issue of slavery, began. The war had a great effect on business in California. Restrictions were placed on the shipping of goods out of the South. This made it very difficult for companies like Levi's to supply its customers with cotton, which came from the South. Some manufacturers found illegal ways to get their cotton. Although Levi refused to do anything that was against the law, he did manage to keep his company going.

After the war, business in California picked up again. In 1866, Levi Strauss & Co. moved into a large warehouse in San Francisco's downtown area. The space was remodeled and included one of the city's first freight elevators. Two years later, however, San Francisco experienced a terrifying and destructive earthquake. The new Strauss warehouse suffered large cracks in the walls. Fortunately, no employees were hurt. The building was repaired and soon was occupied again.

Ideas to Boost Business

Without a doubt, the 1860s brought important changes to American business. But for Levi's company, the most significant change of all came in 1872. That year Levi received a letter from Jacob Davis, a tailor who had come to America from Europe. He was living with his family in Reno, Nevada, where he made work pants out of two types of material supplied by Levi Strauss & Co. One kind was blue denim. The other was a white cotton fabric called duck cloth.

In his letter to Levi, Davis described what happened when a woman recently asked him to make her husband a pair of pants with extra-strong pockets. Davis

To keep up with the increasing demands of the late 1800s, each seamstress at Levi Strauss & Co. had to make five to six pairs of pants each day.

noticed some copper rivets lying near his work table. He had an idea. He used the rivets to fasten the pockets. The rivets proved to be much stronger than thread. Now Davis was being flooded with orders for more pants with the riveted pockets.

Davis's English was very poor, but Levi understood his meaning. Davis wrote:

> The secratt of them pents is the Rivits that I put in those Pockets, and I found the demand so large that I cannot make them up fast enough. I charge for the Duck $3.00 and for the Blue $2.50 a pear. My nabors are getting yealouse of these

success and unless I secure it by Petent Papers it will soon become a general thing. Everybody will make them up and thare will be no money in it.

Davis offered Levi a deal. Davis would go into business with him and make the riveted work pants, if Levi would pay the $68 fee to apply for a patent (governmental permission to produce and sell an invention). Davis sent Levi two pairs of the pants with the rivets. Levi was impressed and agreed to the deal. Serious obstacles were yet to come, however.

To obtain a patent, Davis had to explain how his pants were different from anything ever made before. His first application was rejected. The government claimed that rivets had already been used in a similar way on Civil War uniforms. Davis was not discouraged. And after ten months of rejection, he finally convinced the patent office that his idea was indeed new. The patent was granted.

Davis and his family moved to San Francisco. There he became head foreman for Levi Strauss & Co. Within a year, about 20,000 pairs of riveted jeans had been made and sold. Sales were so good that in 1876 Levi opened a factory in New York City.

This way, people in the East would get their pants more quickly.

In 1873, Levi Strauss & Co. introduced a special design, or trademark, for its jeans. On the back pockets, two arcs were sewn in orange thread. (Orange was chosen to match the color of the copper rivets.) Later, in 1886, another trademark—a leather patch—was added. The patch showed two horses trying to pull apart a pair of Levi's jeans. The company wanted to show just how tough its fabric really was. It offered a free pair of jeans to any customer whose Levi's ever ripped.

Whenever Levi saw a chance for growth, he grabbed it. So, when the Mission and Pacific Woolen Mills announced it was for sale in 1875, Levi bought it. This was the mill where Levi Strauss & Co. purchased its woolen blankets and other materials. By owning the mill, the company would be able to manufacture its own goods at a lower cost. Levi's company was also now making coats, jackets, vests, and shirts.

A Just Boss

As sales at Levi's company increased, so did the number of workers. Seamstresses each made five or six pairs of pants daily. For their labor, Levi paid them three dollars a day. At the time, these were good wages.

Levi believed in paying fair wages to everyone who worked for him. This included the Chinese, who were being paid only pennies a day by other San Francisco business owners.

After the railroad was completed in 1869, many people found themselves out of work. Since the Chinese were willing to work for low wages just to survive, there were fewer jobs for Americans. As a result, there were some Americans who began to resent the Chinese presence in California. In 1877, they robbed and burned Chinese-run stores and businesses.

Levi Strauss felt sorry for the Chinese, but he also felt sorry for the many Americans who were out of work. Levi Strauss & Co. advertised that it used "white labor only" to manufacture its goods. The only Chinese employee was a fabric cutter. He was able to cut through thick material that other workers could not. Levi was not entirely happy with his decision, but he refused to take advantage of his Chinese employee. He paid his Chinese cutter what he would have paid a white person.

5

Leaving a Legacy

"My happiness lies in my routine work." The last half of the 1800s brought great prosperity to Levi Strauss & Co. But for Levi personally, there was also great sadness. In 1867, his half sister, Mathilde, died. Her husband, William Sahlein, now a partner in the company, was left to raise their three children.

In 1874, Levi's brother-in-law David Stern also died. This was a tremendous blow to Levi. Over the years, he and David had grown very close as partners. David, who had been married to Levi's sister Fanny, left eight children. Levi made sure all would become a part of the company.

Even as an important businessperson, Levi devoted much of his time and money to helping others.

The oldest son, Jacob, began working in the San Francisco store. Eventually, the other Stern children would also join the business.

After her husband died, Fanny married William Sahlein. The Strauss-Stern-Sahlein household now totaled 14. Levi, who had never married, had always lived with his sister Fanny. Now Fanny and her children, William and his children, and Levi were all under one roof. They moved to a larger house on San Francisco's Leavenworth Street, to make room for everyone.

Having no wife or children of his own, Levi devoted nearly all his time to the business. Every morning he visited the factory.

In the afternoon, he often attended business meetings. And at the end of the day, he reviewed sales figures with his bookkeeper. Yet despite his wealth and importance, Levi remained friendly and informal—always making it a point to stop and chat with customers.

Other Ventures

After making sizable profits, Levi began to invest in real estate. He purchased several buildings in the downtown San Francisco area and soon gained a reputation as a successful property dealer.

Levi also became active with various institutions and causes. He spent time as treasurer of the San Francisco Board of Trade. He worked to get the U.S. government to build a canal in Central America. Levi felt a canal was desperately needed, recalling how he had been forced years earlier to detour widely to get from New York to California. Eventually, in 1914, the Panama Canal was completed.

Not all of Levi's business efforts were entirely successful, however. One major disappointment occurred in 1891. That year, Levi and 40 other business investors tried to create their own railroad company.

They felt that existing railroad owners were charging too much for goods to be shipped to the East. Each investor put up $25,000 in an effort to establish an independent rail system. It succeeded for a short while. But soon, it was sold to another railroad company without the consent of many of the investors, including Levi. Frustrated, Levi eventually gave up his claim in the project. It was one of the few instances when his business sense failed him.

Pet Charities

Levi grew to be a multimillionaire. But he was always very generous with his wealth. Among his favorite charities was the Eureka Benevolent Society, which offered aid to the needy Jews of San Francisco. He also gave to the Pacific Hebrew Orphan Asylum and Home. And he helped to build Temple Emanuel, one of San Francisco's first synagogues.

Levi did not give only to Jewish causes. He donated to Catholic and Protestant charities as well. He took a special interest in helping children, perhaps because he never had any himself. Because he felt it was important, Levi created scholarships for students at the University of California.

In the mid-1800s, Levi Strauss & Co. moved its operations and headquarters to the downtown San Francisco area. Here, some of Levi's many employees pose proudly for a portrait.

As the end of the century approached, Levi's health forced him to slow down. He eventually turned over store operations to four of the Stern children. Levi continued to remain active in the business until a week before his death. He said the following in a newspaper interview in 1895:

I don't believe that a man who once forms the habit of being busy can retire and be contented. My happiness lies in my routine work....I do not think large fortunes cause happiness to their owners, for immediately those who possess

Since the 1930s and 1940s, Levi's products have been some of the most popular in America. Even today, people continue to flock to stores that sell Levi's pants and jeans.

them become slaves to their wealth. They must devote their lives to caring for their possessions. I don't think money brings friends to its owners. In fact, often the result is quite the contrary.

Levi proved that money could indeed do lots of good. He had learned the value of a dollar, having arrived in America himself with almost no money at all. His was a story of true success. Levi left a legacy of good deeds and charity that continue to benefit others to this day.

The Tradition Lives On

On September 26, 1902, Levi Strauss died in his sleep at the age of 73. His death touched not only his immediate family and friends, but all merchants in San Francisco as well. Many of them closed their shops to attend Levi's funeral. He was buried in a cemetery just outside San Francisco.

Even after Levi's death, Levi Strauss & Co. remained a family operation. The Stern brothers made all the business decisions. Jacob Davis's son also joined the firm, filling the position of production supervisor when his father retired. Not until 1981 did Levi Strauss & Co. have a president who came from outside the family.

In many ways, Levi Strauss & Co. has changed little since Levi's death. The denim jeans that made Levi famous have changed little over the years. At one point, complaints were received that the rivets on the back pockets were scratching saddles and chairs. As a result, those rivets were removed. But the front-pocket rivets remain to this day. In 1936, a small red tag was added on all Levi's jeans and jackets as part of the company trademark. But the orange arcs and leather patch can still be found. The Levi's jeans that were listed in the 1890 company catalog as item 501, remain "Levi's 501" today.

Since Levi's passing in 1902, Levi Strauss & Co. has continued to grow, even in the face of disaster. In 1906, San Francisco experienced its worst earthquake ever. One of the Strauss company's buildings was completely destroyed, and another was badly damaged. Business operations had to be moved to one of the Stern brothers' homes until the store and factory could be rebuilt. During that period, employees were paid, even if they couldn't work because of the damage. No doubt Uncle Levi would have been pleased with that decision.

The company also managed to survive the Great Depression that followed the stock-market crash of 1929. During World War II, Levi Strauss & Co. became one of the first American businesses to employ minorities in its factories. The sign that once advertised "White Labor Only" now proudly announced "We Hire Freely."

Today, Levi Strauss & Co. is one of the largest clothing manufacturers in the world. Over 30,000 people work for the company, which sells in approximately 40,000 retail stores around the world. Most importantly, the firm continues to maintain a strong reputation—as strong as the jeans that first made it famous. Levi Strauss & Co. is known for its excellence, fair dealing, and generosity. That is the legacy that young Loeb Strauss, a penniless peddler from Bavaria, left for future generations.

Glossary

denim A heavy cotton material used to make jeans.

dry goods Fabrics and clothing.

duck cloth A strong, heavy white cotton fabric.

Great Depression A time in the 1930s when many people were out of work and there was a sharp decline in economic activity.

kosher Allowed to be eaten or used, according to the religious laws of the Jews.

patent A document issued by the government that allows a person the exclusive right to make, use, or sell an invention or process for a certain period of time.

retail The sale of goods in small quantities to consumers.

rivet A metal fastener used on clothing to hold two or more pieces of material together.

Sabbath The seventh day of the week, observed from Friday evening to Saturday evening as a day of rest and worship by Jews.

scholarship A gift of money given to a student for education.

synagogue A Jewish house of worship.

trademark A word, symbol, or design used by a manufacturer to let the consumer know that the product is original.

wholesale The sale of goods in large quantities to businesses.

Further Reading

Henry, Sandra, and Taitz, Emily. *Levi Strauss—Everyone Wears His Name: A Biography*. New York: Macmillan, 1990.

Reimers, David. *Immigrant Experience*. Broomall, PA: Chelsea House, 1989.

Van Steenwyk, Elizabeth. *California Gold Rush: West with the Forty-Niners*. New York: Franklin Watts, 1991.

Van Steenwyk, Elizabeth. *Levi Strauss: The Blue Jeans Man*. New York: Walker, 1988.

Index

Photo Credits:
Cover: Courtesy of Levi Strauss & Co.; p. 4: Courtesy of
Levi Strauss & Co.; p. 9: The Bettmann Archive; p. 15:
Culver Pictures, Inc.; p. 23: Courtesy of Levi Strauss &
Co.; p. 28: Courtesy of Levi Strauss & Co.; p. 30: Culver
Pictures, Inc.; p. 38: Courtesy of Levi Strauss & Co.; p. 41:
Courtesy of Levi Strauss & Co.; p. 42: Courtesy of Levi
Strauss & Co.

Illustrations by Dick Smolinski.